THE PIZZA COOKBOOK

Edited by

Norma MacMillan

Contents

NOTES

Standard spoon measurements are used in all recipes
1 tablespoon = one 15 ml spoon
1 teaspoon = one 5 ml spoon
All spoon measures are level.

Fresh herbs are used unless otherwise stated. If unobtainable, substitute a bouquet garni of the equivalent dried herbs, or use dried herbs instead but halve the quantities stated.

Ovens and grills (broilers) should be preheated to the specified temperature or heat setting.

For all recipes, quantities are given in metric, imperial and American measures. Follow one set of measures only, because they are not interchangeable.

This edition first published 1981 by
Octopus Books Limited,
59 Grosvenor Street, London W1

© 1981 Octopus Books Limited

ISBN 0 7064 1512 4

Produced by Mandarin Publishers Ltd
22a Westlands Road,
Quarry Bay, Hong Kong
Printed in Hong Kong   Cover photography by Paul Williams

Frontispiece PASTA PIZZA *(page 70) (Photograph: The Pasta Information Centre)*

INTRODUCTION

To an Italian, a pizza is a pie – savoury or sweet, open or covered, with a base of pastry or bread dough. We take the word pizza to mean a flat, round, open pie. But however it is defined, a pizza makes an economical and filling meal, and gives the cook the opportunity to experiment with whatever toppings imagination suggests.

Of the many variations of pizza, the best known is Neapolitan, which has a topping of tomatoes, anchovies, black olives and Mozzarella cheese on a bread dough base. You will find this in every *pizzeria*, or 'pizza parlour', where it may even be cooked in a traditional brick bread oven. You'll find it, too, in the supermarket in packaged pizza mixes or frozen, ready for reheating. But making a pizza at home is no trouble, whether it be on a bread, scone (biscuit) or pastry base, and it's certainly less expensive than buying someone else's effort. After all, the pizza came about as a method of using up leftover bread dough to make a cheap meal.

The recipes in this book comprise both traditional and unusual toppings, using meat and poultry – fresh or leftover, canned and smoked fish, shellfish, all sorts of vegetables and fruit, eggs, many varieties of cheese, and herbs and other seasonings. There are also some ideas for quick pizzas to be made up on a base of toast or an English muffin. And, finally, some 'near' pizzas: using traditional pizza flavours, these have such bases as rice, aubergine (eggplant) slices, fried potato and hamburgers.

Homemade pizzas on a yeast dough base, baked or unbaked, can be frozen successfully for up to 1 month. Add the topping, checking first that all ingredients are suitable for freezing (anchovies become too strong during freezing so should be added when reheating), then open (flash) freeze before wrapping in freezer foil or a freezer bag. Bake the pizza from frozen in a preheated moderately hot oven (200°C/400°F, Gas Mark 6) for about 20 minutes for a baked pizza, and 30 to 35 minutes for an unbaked pizza.

PIZZA BASES

Wholemeal Scone (Wholewheat Biscuit) Pizza Dough

METRIC/IMPERIAL
200 g/7 oz fine wholemeal flour
25 g/1 oz soya flour
pinch of sea salt
1 teaspoon baking powder
25 g/1 oz butter or margarine
25 g/1 oz sugar
175 ml/6 fl oz milk or buttermilk
beaten egg to glaze (optional)

AMERICAN
1¾ cups fine wholewheat flour
¼ cup soy flour
pinch of coarse dairy salt
1 teaspoon baking powder
2 tablespoons butter or margarine
2 tablespoons sugar
¾ cup milk or buttermilk
beaten egg to glaze (optional)

Sift the flours, salt and baking powder into a mixing bowl. Rub in the butter or margarine until the mixture resembles breadcrumbs, then stir in the sugar. Bind to a soft dough with the milk or buttermilk. Use as directed in the recipe.

If quick pizzas are being made, using baked scone (biscuit) bases, brush the rounds with beaten egg and bake in a preheated hot oven (230°C/450°F, Gas Mark 8) for 10 to 15 minutes or until risen and golden brown.

Note: Use this dough in any recipe calling for basic scone (biscuit) pizza dough.

8   SWEETCORN AND BROAD (LIMA) BEAN FRITTER PIZZA
(page 71) (Photograph: Canned Food Advisory Service)

Basic Yeast Pizza Dough

METRIC/IMPERIAL

225 g/8 oz plain or wholemeal flour
1 teaspoon salt
15 g/½ oz fresh yeast, or 1 teaspoon
  dried yeast and ¼ teaspoon caster
  sugar
150 ml/¼ pint lukewarm water
25 g/1 oz butter or lard, softened,
  or 2 tablespoons olive oil

AMERICAN

2 cups all-purpose or wholewheat flour
1 teaspoon salt
½ oz cake compressed yeast, or
  ½ package active dry yeast and
  ¼ teaspoon sugar
⅔ cup lukewarm water
2 tablespoons softened butter,
  shortening or olive oil

Sift the flour and salt into a mixing bowl; if using wholemeal (wholewheat) flour you may prefer not to sift out the bran. If using fresh (compressed) yeast, cream it with the water and leave in a warm place until frothy. For dried yeast, dissolve the sugar in the water, sprinkle over the yeast, stir and leave in a warm place for 10 to 15 minutes or until frothy.

Stir the yeast liquid into the flour, then mix to a soft dough with the butter, lard (shortening) or oil. Cover the bowl and leave the dough to rise in a warm place for about 45 minutes.

Knock back (punch down) the dough, then use as directed in the recipe.

Basic Scone (Biscuit) Pizza Dough

METRIC/IMPERIAL

225 g/8 oz self-raising flour, or plain
  flour and 2 teaspoons baking powder
½ teaspoon salt
50 g/2 oz butter or margarine
150 ml/¼ pint milk

AMERICAN

2 cups self-rising flour, or all-purpose
  flour and 2 teaspoons baking powder
½ teaspoon salt
4 tablespoons butter or margarine
⅔ cup milk

Sift the flour (or flour and baking powder) and salt into a mixing bowl. Rub in the butter or margarine until the mixture resembles breadcrumbs. Bind to a soft dough with the milk, then knead until smooth. Use as directed in the recipe.

Rich Yeast Pizza Dough

METRIC/IMPERIAL
225 g/8 oz flour
½ teaspoon salt
15 g/½ oz fresh yeast, or 1 teaspoon
  dried yeast and ¼ teaspoon caster
  sugar
about 5 tablespoons lukewarm milk
1 to 2 eggs, beaten
50 g/2 oz butter or margarine,
  softened

AMERICAN
2 cups flour
½ teaspoon salt
½ oz cake compressed yeast, or
  ½ package active dry yeast and
  ¼ teaspoon sugar
about 5 tablespoons lukewarm milk
1 to 2 eggs, beaten
4 tablespoons butter or margarine,
  softened

Sift the flour and salt into a mixing bowl. If using fresh (compressed) yeast, cream it with the milk and leave in a warm place until frothy. For dried yeast, dissolve the sugar in the milk, sprinkle over the yeast, stir and leave in a warm place for 10 to 15 minutes or until frothy.

Stir the yeast liquid into the flour, then mix in enough egg to make a soft dough. Beat in the butter or margarine. Cover the bowl and leave the dough to rise in a warm place for about 45 minutes.

Knock back (punch down) the dough, then use as directed in the recipe.

Note: Use this dough in any recipe calling for basic yeast pizza dough.

Tomato Sauce

METRIC/IMPERIAL
2 tablespoons olive oil
1 large onion, chopped
1 garlic clove, crushed (optional)
1 × 400 g/14 oz can tomatoes
1 teaspoon sugar
1 tablespoon tomato purée
good pinch of dried Italian seasoning
  or oregano
salt
freshly ground black pepper

AMERICAN
2 tablespoons olive oil
1 large onion, chopped
1 garlic clove, crushed (optional)
1 × 14 oz can tomatoes
1 teaspoon sugar
1 tablespoon tomato paste
large pinch of dried Italian seasoning
  or oregano
salt
freshly ground black pepper

Heat the oil in a saucepan, add the onion and garlic, if used, and cook gently until softened. Stir in the remaining ingredients with salt and pepper to taste and simmer, stirring occasionally, until the sauce is thick. Adjust the seasoning and use as required.

VEGETABLE PIZZAS

Mushroom and Green Pepper Pizza

METRIC/IMPERIAL
1 quantity basic yeast pizza dough
1 quantity tomato sauce
25 g/1 oz butter or margarine
2 tablespoons oil
1 garlic clove, crushed
225 g/8 oz button mushrooms
2 green peppers, cored, seeded and
 cut into rings
8 anchovy fillets to garnish

AMERICAN
1 quantity basic yeast pizza dough
1 quantity tomato sauce
2 tablespoons butter or margarine
2 tablespoons oil
1 garlic clove, crushed
½ lb button mushrooms
2 green peppers, cored, seeded and
 cut into rings
8 anchovy fillets to garnish

Roll out the risen dough to one large round about 1 cm/½ inch thick. Transfer to a greased baking sheet, and push up the edge of the round to make a rim. Spread the tomato sauce over the dough round, then bake in a preheated moderately hot oven (200°C/400°F, Gas Mark 6) for 20 minutes.

Meanwhile, melt the butter or margarine with the oil in a frying pan (skillet). Add the garlic and stir it into the fat, then add the mushrooms. Cook until they are just tender. Remove from the heat and keep warm.

Arrange the pepper rings around the edge of the dough round and garnish with the anchovy fillets. Return to the oven and bake for a further 10 to 15 minutes or until the pizza base is cooked. Pile the mushrooms in the centre and serve.

Serves 2 to 4

MUSHROOM AND GREEN PEPPER PIZZA *(Photograph: Mushroom Growers' Association)*

Mushroom Pizza

METRIC/IMPERIAL

1 quantity basic yeast pizza dough
4 tablespoons olive oil
2 large onions, sliced
2 garlic cloves, crushed
350 g/12 oz mushrooms, sliced
salt
freshly ground black pepper
2 tablespoons chopped fresh mixed
  herbs

AMERICAN

1 quantity basic yeast pizza dough
¼ cup olive oil
2 large onions, sliced
2 garlic cloves, crushed
¾ lb mushrooms, sliced
salt
freshly ground black pepper
2 tablespoons chopped fresh mixed
  herbs

Roll out the risen dough to one large or two smaller rounds about 1cm/½ inch thick and transfer to a greased baking sheet. Push up the edge of the round(s) to make a rim.

Heat the oil in a frying pan (skillet), add the onions and garlic and fry until softened. Add the mushrooms and cook until just tender. Season to taste with salt and pepper and mix in the herbs. Spread the mushroom mixture over the dough round(s), then leave in a warm place to rise for 10 to 15 minutes.

Bake in a preheated moderately hot oven (200°C/400°F, Gas Mark 6) for 30 to 35 minutes.
Serves 2 to 4

Tomato and Artichoke Pizza

METRIC/IMPERIAL

225 g/8 oz frozen puff pastry, thawed
1 × 225 g/8 oz can artichoke hearts,
  drained and halved
1 × 400 g/14 oz can tomatoes,
  drained and chopped
25 g/1 oz Parmesan cheese, grated
1 garlic clove, crushed
2 tablespoons chopped parsley
1 tablespoon oil

AMERICAN

½ lb frozen puff pastry, thawed
1 × ½ lb can artichoke hearts,
  drained and halved
1 × 14 oz can tomatoes,
  drained and chopped
¼ cup grated Parmesan cheese
1 garlic clove, crushed
2 tablespoons chopped parsley
1 tablespoon oil

Roll out the dough and use to line a 20 cm/8 inch flan ring (shallow pie pan). Arrange the artichoke hearts in the pastry case and spread over the tomatoes. Sprinkle with the cheese. Mix together the garlic and parsley and scatter over the top, then dribble over the oil.

Bake in a preheated hot oven (220°C/425°F, Gas Mark 7) for 20 to 25 minutes.
Serves 2 to 4

Aubergine (Eggplant) Pizza

METRIC/IMPERIAL
1 large aubergine, sliced
salt
4 to 6 tablespoons oil
1 quantity basic yeast pizza dough
1 quantity tomato sauce
freshly ground black pepper
100 g/4 oz Mozzarella cheese, sliced
2 tablespoons grated Parmesan cheese

AMERICAN
1 large eggplant, sliced
salt
4 to 6 tablespoons oil
1 quantity basic yeast pizza dough
1 quantity tomato sauce
freshly ground black pepper
¼ lb Mozzarella cheese, sliced
2 tablespoons grated Parmesan cheese

Sprinkle the aubergine (eggplant) slices with salt and leave for 20 minutes, then rinse and pat dry with paper towels. Heat 4 tablespoons of the oil in a frying pan (skillet), add the aubergine (eggplant) slices in batches and brown on both sides. Add more oil to the pan as necessary. Drain the aubergine (eggplant) slices on paper towels.

Roll out the risen dough to one large or two smaller rounds about 1 cm/½ inch thick and transfer to a greased baking sheet. Push up the edge of the round(s) to make a rim.

Spread the tomato sauce over the dough round(s), then arrange the aubergine (eggplant) slices on top. Cover with the Mozzarella and sprinkle over the Parmesan. Leave in a warm place to rise for 10 to 15 minutes.

Bake in a preheated moderately hot oven (200°C/400°F, Gas Mark 6) for 30 to 35 minutes.

Serves 2 to 4

Mushroom and Tomato Pizza Plait (Braid)

METRIC/IMPERIAL

basic yeast pizza dough, made with
  350 g/12 oz flour and 200 ml/⅓ pint
  water
25 g/1 oz butter or margarine
225 g/8 oz button mushrooms, sliced
1 garlic clove, crushed
4 tomatoes, thinly sliced
salt
freshly ground black pepper
100 g/4 oz Cheddar cheese, grated
milk to glaze

AMERICAN

basic yeast pizza dough, made with
  3 cups flour and ¾ cup plus
  2 tablespoons water
2 tablespoons butter or margarine
½ lb button mushrooms, sliced
1 garlic clove, crushed
4 tomatoes, thinly sliced
salt
freshly ground black pepper
1 cup grated Cheddar cheese
milk to glaze

Break off one-third of the risen dough and set aside. Roll out the remaining dough to a round about 28 cm/11 inches in diameter and transfer to a greased baking sheet. Divide the reserved portion of dough into three and shape into three long thin strands. Plait (braid) the strands. Dampen the edge of the dough round and gently press the plait (braid) onto it. Leave to rise in a warm place for 10 to 15 minutes.

Meanwhile, melt the butter or margarine in a frying pan (skillet), add the mushrooms and garlic and fry until just tender. Drain well.

Arrange the sliced tomatoes on the dough round, inside the plait (braid). Season with salt and pepper. Scatter over the mushrooms and sprinkle with the cheese. Brush the plait (braid) with milk, then bake in a preheated moderately hot oven (200°C/400°F, Gas Mark 6) for about 30 minutes.

Serves 4 to 6

MUSHROOM AND TOMATO PIZZA PLAIT (BRAID)
(Photograph: The Home Baking Bureau)

Pan-fried Tomato Pizza

METRIC/IMPERIAL

Dough:

25 g/1 oz butter or margarine,
 softened
1 teaspoon yeast extract
1 × 184 g/6½ oz packet scone mix
4 tablespoons water
2 tablespoons oil

Topping:

1 quantity tomato sauce
1 teaspoon yeast extract
50 g/2 oz cheese, grated

AMERICAN

Dough:

2 tablespoons butter or margarine,
 softened
1 teaspoon brewer's yeast
1½ cups biscuit mix
¼ cup water
2 tablespoons oil

Topping:

1 quantity tomato sauce
1 teaspoon brewer's yeast
½ cup grated cheese

First make the dough. Mix the butter or margarine with the yeast extract (brewer's yeast), then rub into the scone (biscuit) mix. Bind to a soft dough with the water. Roll out into a 20 cm/8 inch round.

Heat the oil in a frying pan (skillet) and cook the dough round until the underside is golden brown. Turn over and cook the other side.

Mix the tomato sauce with the yeast extract (brewer's yeast) and spread over the dough round. Sprinkle with the cheese. Place under a preheated grill (broiler) and cook until the cheese has melted.

Serves 2 to 4

Herby Olive Pizza Tart

METRIC/IMPERIAL

rich shortcrust pastry dough, made
 with 225 g/8 oz flour, 100 g/4 oz
 fat and 2 eggs
double quantity tomato sauce
3 to 4 tablespoons chopped fresh herbs
about 25 green olives, stoned
1 teaspoon oil

AMERICAN

rich pie pastry dough, made with
 2 cups flour, ½ cup fat and 2 eggs
double quantity tomato sauce
3 to 4 tablespoons chopped fresh herbs
about 25 green olives, pitted
1 teaspoon oil

Roll out the dough and use to line a 20 cm/8 inch round flan tin (pie pan). Bake blind (unfilled) in a preheated moderately hot oven (190°C/375°F, Gas Mark 5) for 15 minutes.

Pour the tomato sauce into the pastry case, scatter over the herbs and arrange the olives on top. Sprinkle with the oil. Bake in a moderate oven (180°C/350°F, Gas Mark 4) for 10 to 15 minutes.

Serves 2 to 4

Spinach Pizza

METRIC/IMPERIAL

25 g/1 oz butter or margarine
2 tablespoons olive oil
1 garlic clove, crushed
1 onion, finely chopped
750 g/1½ lb spinach, torn into small
  pieces
salt
freshly ground black pepper
1 quantity basic yeast pizza dough
100 g/4 oz Fontina or Bel Paese
  cheese, cut into strips
3 tablespoons grated Parmesan cheese

AMERICAN

2 tablespoons butter or margarine
2 tablespoons olive oil
1 garlic clove, crushed
1 onion, finely chopped
1½ lb spinach, torn into small
  pieces
salt
freshly ground black pepper
1 quantity basic yeast pizza dough
¼ lb Fontina or Bel Paese cheese,
  cut into strips
3 tablespoons grated Parmesan cheese

Melt the butter or margarine with the oil in a saucepan. Add the garlic
and onion and fry until softened. Stir in the spinach and cook gently,
covered, until the spinach is tender and wilted. Stir occasionally so that the
spinach is mixed with the fat. Season to taste with salt and pepper.

Roll out the risen dough to one large or two smaller rounds about
1 cm/½ inch thick and transfer to a greased baking sheet. Push up the edge
of the round(s) to make a rim. Spread the spinach mixture over the dough
round(s), then make a lattice of Fontina or Bel Paese cheese strips over the
top. Sprinkle with the Parmesan. Leave in a warm place to rise for 10 to
15 minutes.

Bake in a preheated moderately hot oven (200°C/400°F, Gas Mark 6)
for 30 to 35 minutes.
Serves 2 to 4

MEAT PIZZAS

Salami and Anchovy Pizza

METRIC/IMPERIAL
1 quantity basic yeast pizza dough
1 quantity tomato sauce
100 g/4 oz salami, thinly sliced
100 g/4 oz Mozzarella cheese,
  thinly sliced
1 × 50 g/2 oz can anchovy fillets,
  drained
10 black olives to garnish
1 tablespoon olive oil

AMERICAN
1 quantity basic yeast pizza dough
1 quantity tomato sauce
$\frac{1}{4}$ lb salami, thinly sliced
$\frac{1}{4}$ lb Mozzarella cheese, thinly
  sliced
1 × 2 oz can anchovy fillets,
  drained
10 black olives to garnish
1 tablespoon olive oil

Roll out the risen dough to one large or two smaller rounds about
1 cm/$\frac{1}{2}$ inch thick. Transfer to a greased baking sheet and push up the
edge of the round(s) to make a rim.

Spread half the tomato sauce over the dough round(s), cover with the
salami slices, then add the rest of the tomato sauce. Arrange the cheese
slices over the top. Make a lattice with the anchovy fillets and garnish
with the olives. Sprinkle over the oil.

Bake in a preheated moderately hot oven (200°C/400°F, Gas Mark 6)
for 30 to 35 minutes.
Serves 2 to 4

SALAMI AND ANCHOVY PIZZA *(Photograph: RHM Foods Ltd)*

Layered Sausagemeat and Cheese Pizza

METRIC/IMPERIAL
225 g/8 oz spicy sausagemeat
1 × 400 g/14 oz can tomatoes
1 quantity basic yeast pizza dough
salt
freshly ground black pepper
100 g/4 oz Mozzarella cheese,
  thinly sliced
4 tablespoons tomato purée
1 garlic clove, crushed
1½ teaspoons dried Italian seasoning
25 g/1 oz Romano cheese, grated

AMERICAN
½ lb spicy sausagemeat
1 × 14 oz can tomatoes
1 quantity basic yeast pizza dough
salt
freshly ground black pepper
¼ lb Mozzarella cheese, thinly
  sliced
¼ cup tomato paste
1 garlic clove, crushed
1½ teaspoons dried Italian seasoning
¼ cup grated Romano cheese

Place the sausagemeat in a dry frying pan and fry until crumbly and browned. Drain on paper towels.

Drain the tomatoes, reserving 4 tablespoons (¼ cup) of the juice. Chop the tomatoes.

Roll out the risen dough to one large or two smaller rounds about 1 cm/½ inch thick and transfer to a greased baking sheet. Push up the edge of the round(s) to make a rim. Spread the tomatoes over the dough round(s) and sprinkle with salt and pepper. Cover with the Mozzarella slices and scatter over the sausagemeat.

Mix together the reserved tomato juice, the tomato purée (paste), garlic, Italian seasoning and salt and pepper to taste. Spread over the sausagemeat and sprinkle with the Romano cheese.

Leave in a warm place to rise for 10 to 15 minutes, then bake in a preheated moderately hot oven (200°C/400°F, Gas Mark 6) for 30 to 35 minutes.

Serves 2 to 4

Italian Sausage Pizza

METRIC/IMPERIAL
1 × 300 g/10 oz packet brown bread
  mix, or 1 quantity basic yeast pizza
  dough
1 quantity tomato sauce
100 g/4 oz Italian sausage, chopped
175 g/6 oz Mozzarella cheese, sliced
3 thin slices of cooked ham, cut into
  strips
chopped parsley to garnish

AMERICAN
1 × 10 oz package brown bread mix
  or 1 quantity basic yeast pizza
  dough
1 quantity tomato sauce
$\frac{1}{4}$ lb Italian sausage, chopped
6 oz Mozzarella cheese, sliced
3 thin slices of cooked ham, cut into
  strips
chopped parsley to garnish

If using bread mix, make up with hot water according to the instructions
on the package. Knead for 5 minutes. Roll out the dough to one large or
two smaller rounds about 1 cm/$\frac{1}{2}$ inch thick. Transfer to greased baking
sheets and push up the edge of the round(s) to make a rim. Leave to rise in
a warm place for 30 minutes, then bake the dough round(s) in a preheated
moderately hot oven (200°C/400°F, Gas Mark 6) for 10 minutes.

Spread the tomato sauce over the pizza base. Sprinkle over the sausage
and cover with the cheese. Bake for a further 20 to 25 minutes.

Make a lattice with the ham strips, and sprinkle parsley over the top.

Serves 2 to 4

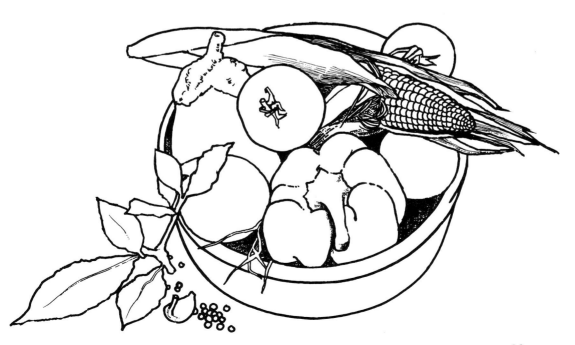

Sausage and Bean Pizza

METRIC/IMPERIAL
5 thin pork or beef sausages
1 quantity basic scone pizza dough
1 × 425 g/15 oz can baked beans
100 g/4 oz mushrooms, sliced
pinch of dried mixed herbs
50 g/2 oz cheese, grated
chopped parsley to garnish

AMERICAN
5 thin pork or beef sausages
1 quantity basic biscuit pizza dough
1 × 15 oz can baked beans
1 cup sliced mushrooms
pinch of dried mixed herbs
½ cup grated cheese
chopped parsley to garnish

Cook the sausages under a preheated grill (broiler) until they are lightly browned on all sides.

Meanwhile, roll out the dough to a round about 1 cm/½ inch thick and transfer it to a greased baking sheet. Push up the edge of the round to make a rim. Spread over the baked beans, then scatter with the mushrooms. Sprinkle with the herbs.

Drain the sausages and arrange them on the pizza base. Scatter over the cheese. Bake in a preheated moderately hot oven (200°C/400°F, Gas Mark 6) for 20 to 25 minutes. Garnish with parsley before serving.

Serves 2 to 4

Prosciutto Pizza

METRIC/IMPERIAL
1 quantity basic yeast pizza dough
4 tablespoons oil
2 large onions, sliced
225 g/8 oz prociutto, cut into thin strips
100 g/4 oz mortadella sausage, cut into thin strips
1 to 2 teaspoons Dijon mustard
salt
freshly ground black pepper

AMERICAN
1 quantity basic yeast pizza dough
¼ cup oil
2 large onions, sliced
½ lb prosciutto, cut into thin strips
¼ lb mortadella sausage, cut into thin strips
1 to 2 teaspoons Dijon mustard
salt
freshly ground black pepper

Roll out the risen dough to one large or two smaller rounds about 1 cm/½ inch thick and transfer to a greased baking sheet. Push up the edge of the round(s) to make a rim.

Heat the oil in a frying pan (skillet), add the onions and fry until golden brown. Remove from the heat and mix in the prosciutto, mortadella, mustard and salt and pepper to taste. Spread over the dough round(s), then leave in a warm place to rise for 10 to 15 minutes.

Bake in a preheated moderately hot oven (200°C/400°F, Gas Mark 6) for 30 to 35 minutes.

Serves 2 to 4

SAUSAGE AND BEAN PIZZA *(Photograph: British Sausage Bureau)*

Cheese and Ham Pizza

METRIC/IMPERIAL
1 quantity basic yeast pizza dough
225 g/8 oz Ricotta or curd cheese
2 tablespoons grated Parmesan cheese
1 egg, beaten
50 g/2 oz cooked ham, diced
salt
freshly ground black pepper

AMERICAN
1 quantity basic yeast pizza dough
½ lb Ricotta or small curd cottage cheese
2 tablespoons grated Parmesan cheese
1 egg, beaten
¼ cup diced cooked ham
salt
freshly ground black pepper

Roll out the risen dough to one large or two smaller rounds about 1 cm/ ½ inch thick and transfer to a greased baking sheet. Push up the edge of the round(s) to make a rim.

Beat together the cheeses with the egg, then mix in the ham and season to taste with salt and pepper. Spread the cheese mixture over the dough round(s) and leave in a warm place to rise for 10 to 15 minutes.

Bake in a preheated moderately hot oven (200°C/400°F, Gas Mark 6) for 30 to 35 minutes.

Serves 2 to 4

Pepperoni Pizza

METRIC/IMPERIAL
1 quantity basic yeast pizza dough
1 quantity tomato sauce
100 g/4 oz mushrooms, sliced
melted butter or margarine
225 g/8 oz pepperoni sausage, sliced
1 tablespoon aniseed (optional)

AMERICAN
1 quantity basic yeast pizza dough
1 quantity tomato sauce
1 cup sliced mushrooms
melted butter or margarine
½ lb pepperoni sausage, sliced
1 tablespoon aniseed (optional)

Roll out the risen dough to one large or two smaller rounds about 1 cm/ ½ inch thick and transfer to a greased baking sheet. Push up the edge of the round(s) to make a rim.

Spread the tomato sauce over the dough round(s) and scatter over the mushrooms. Brush them with a little melted butter or margarine, then cover with the pepperoni slices. Sprinkle with the aniseed, if used. Leave in a warm place to rise for 10 to 15 minutes.

Bake in a preheated moderately hot oven (200°C/400°F, Gas Mark 6) for 30 to 35 minutes.

Serves 2 to 4

Liver Pâté and Sausage Pan Pizza

METRIC/IMPERIAL
100 g/4 oz flour
pinch of salt
1 teaspoon baking powder
3 tablespoons oil
Topping:
100 g/4 oz liver pâté
1 × 225 g/8 oz can tomatoes,
  drained and chopped
100 g/4 oz beer sausage, cut into strips
50 g/2 oz Cheddar cheese, grated
25 g/1 oz Parmesan cheese, grated
chopped parsley to garnish

AMERICAN
1 cup flour
pinch of salt
1 teaspoon baking powder
3 tablespoons oil
Topping:
¼ lb liver pâté
1 × ½ lb can tomatoes, drained and
  chopped
4 oz beer sausage, cut into strips
½ cup grated Cheddar cheese
¼ cup grated Parmesan cheese
chopped parsley to garnish

Sift the flour, salt and baking powder into a bowl and work in enough water to make a fairly firm dough. Knead lightly, then roll out the dough to a thin round about 18 cm/7 inches in diameter.

Heat the oil in a frying pan (skillet) large enough to take the dough round. Put in the dough and cook for 5 minutes or until the underside is golden brown. Turn the pizza base over and spread over the pâté. Cover with the tomatoes, then arrange the sausage strips on top. Sprinkle with the cheeses.

Cover the pan and continue cooking for about 10 minutes or until the cheeses have melted. Pop under a preheated grill (broiler) just to brown the cheese, then sprinkle with parsley.

Serves 1 to 2

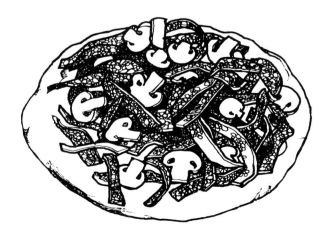

Liver Sausage and Bratwurst Pizza

METRIC/IMPERIAL
100 g/4 oz bratwurst
rich shortcrust pastry dough, made
* with 175 g/6 oz flour, 75 g/3 oz*
* fat and 1 egg*
1 tablespoon oil
1 onion, sliced
100 g/4 oz liver sausage
50 g/2 oz Cheddar cheese, grated
2 tomatoes, sliced
1 teaspoon dried thyme

AMERICAN
$\frac{1}{4}$ lb bratwurst
rich pie pastry dough, made with
* $1\frac{1}{2}$ cups flour, 6 tablespoons fat*
* and 1 egg*
1 tablespoon oil
1 onion, sliced
$\frac{1}{4}$ lb liver sausage
$\frac{1}{2}$ cup grated Cheddar cheese
2 tomatoes, sliced
1 teaspoon dried thyme

Cook the bratwurst under a preheated grill (broiler) until they are browned on all sides. Remove from the heat and cut in halves lengthways.

Roll out the dough to a round about 23 cm/9 inches in diameter. Transfer to a greased baking sheet. Push up the edge of the round to make a rim.

Heat the oil in a frying pan (skillet), add the onion and fry until softened. Spread the onion over the dough round, then cover with the liver sausage followed by the cheese. Arrange the bratwurst strips and tomato slices on top. Sprinkle with the thyme.

Bake in a preheated hot oven (220°C/425°F, Gas Mark 7) for 30 to 35 minutes.

Serves 3 to 4

From top left, clockwise: LIVER SAUSAGE AND BRATWURST PIZZA, MINI SALAMI PIZZAS *(page 54)* and LIVER PATE AND SAUSAGE PAN PIZZA *(page 27) (Photograph: Mattesons)*

Meatball Pizza

METRIC/IMPERIAL
2 slices of bread, crusts removed
milk
225 g/8 oz pie veal
1 garlic clove
small bunch of parsley
1 lemon rind strip
1 egg, beaten
25 g/1 oz Parmesan cheese, grated
pinch of grated nutmeg
salt
freshly ground black pepper
flour for coating
oil for frying
1 quantity tomato sauce
1 quantity basic yeast pizza dough

AMERICAN
2 slices of bread, crusts removed
milk
$\frac{1}{2}$ lb veal stew meat
1 garlic clove
small bunch of parsley
1 lemon rind strip
1 egg, beaten
$\frac{1}{4}$ cup grated Parmesan cheese
pinch of grated nutmeg
salt
freshly ground black pepper
flour for coating
oil for frying
1 quantity tomato sauce
1 quantity basic yeast pizza dough

Soak the bread in milk, then squeeze out all excess milk. Mince (grind) the veal, bread, garlic, parsley and lemon rind twice, then work in the egg, 2 tablespoons of the cheese, the nutmeg and salt and pepper to taste. Shape the mixture into small balls and coat in flour.

Heat the oil in a frying pan, add the meatballs, in batches, and brown on all sides. Remove the meatballs from the pan as they are browned and drain on paper towels. Mix the meatballs with the tomato sauce.

Roll out the risen dough to one large or two smaller rounds about 1 cm/$\frac{1}{2}$ inch thick. Transfer to a greased baking sheet. Push up the edge of the round(s) to make a rim.

Spread the meatballs and sauce over the dough round(s). Sprinkle over the remaining cheese. Leave in a warm place to rise for 10 to 15 minutes, then bake in a preheated moderately hot oven (200°C/400°F, Gas Mark 6) for 30 to 35 minutes.
Serves 2 to 4

Salami Pastry Pizza

METRIC/IMPERIAL
100 g/4 oz shortcrust pastry mix
100 g/4 oz self-raising flour
pinch of salt
½ teaspoon dried mixed herbs
about 150 ml/¼ pint milk
Topping:
1 quantity tomato sauce
2 tomatoes, skinned and sliced
100 g/4 oz salami, thinly sliced
100 g/4 oz Cheddar cheese, grated
parsley sprig to garnish

AMERICAN
1 cup pie pastry mix
1 cup self-rising flour, sifted
pinch of salt
½ teaspoon dried mixed herbs
about ⅔ cup milk
Topping:
1 quantity tomato sauce
2 tomatoes, skinned and sliced
¼ lb salami, thinly sliced
1 cup grated Cheddar cheese
parsley sprig to garnish

Put the pastry mix, flour, salt, herbs and milk into a bowl and mix to a soft dough. Knead lightly, then roll out to a 25 cm/10 inch round. Transfer to a greased baking sheet and push up the edge of the round to make a rim.

Spread the tomato sauce over the dough round, then arrange the tomatoes and salami on top. Sprinkle with the cheese.

Bake in a preheated moderately hot oven (200°C/400°F, Gas Mark 6) for 25 to 30 minutes. Garnish with a parsley sprig.

Serves 3 to 4

Bacon Pan Pizza

METRIC/IMPERIAL

1 quantity basic scone pizza dough
3 tablespoons oil
8 back bacon rashers, rinded
1 quantity tomato sauce, hot
100 g/4 oz Mozzarella cheese, sliced
parsley sprig to garnish

AMERICAN

1 quantity basic biscuit pizza dough
3 tablespoons oil
8 slices of Canadian bacon
1 quantity tomato sauce, hot
$\frac{1}{4}$ lb Mozzarella cheese, sliced
parsley sprig to garnish

Roll out the dough to one large or two smaller rounds about 1 cm/$\frac{1}{2}$ inch thick. Heat the oil in a frying pan (skillet) large enough to take the dough round. Put in the dough and cook for 5 minutes or until the underside is golden brown.

Meanwhile, grill (broil) the bacon. Drain on paper towels.

Turn the pizza dough base over and spread with the hot tomato sauce. Arrange the bacon on top and cover with the cheese slices.

Cover the pan and continue cooking for about 10 minutes or until the pizza base is cooked through and the cheese has melted. Serve garnished with a parsley sprig.

Serves 2 to 4

BACON PAN PIZZA *(Photograph: The Danish Centre)*

Chicken and Sweetcorn Pizza

METRIC/IMPERIAL

1 × 300 g/10 oz packet brown bread mix, or 1 quantity basic scone pizza dough
25 g/1 oz butter or margarine
25 g/1 oz flour
300 ml/½ pint milk
salt
freshly ground black pepper
175 g/6 oz cooked chicken meat, diced
75 g/3 oz drained canned sweetcorn
75 g/3 oz Cheddar cheese, grated

AMERICAN

1 × 10 oz package brown bread mix, or 1 quantity basic biscuit pizza dough
2 tablespoons butter or margarine
¼ cup flour
1¼ cups milk
salt
freshly ground black pepper
¾ cup diced cooked chicken meat
½ cup drained canned corn kernels
¾ cup grated Cheddar cheese

If using the bread mix, make it up with hot water according to the instructions on the package. Knead for 5 minutes. Roll out the dough to one large or two smaller rounds about 1 cm/½ inch thick. Transfer to greased baking sheets and push up the edge of the round(s) to make a rim. If using bread mix dough, leave to rise in a warm place for 30 minutes.

Meanwhile, melt the butter or margarine in a saucepan, stir in the flour and cook for 1 minute. Gradually stir in the milk and bring to the boil, stirring. Season to taste with salt and pepper, then fold in the chicken and sweetcorn.

Spread the chicken filling over the dough round(s). Bake in a preheated hot oven (230°C/450°F, Gas Mark 8) for 15 minutes, if using bread mix. For a scone (biscuit) base, bake in a moderately hot oven (200°C/400°F, Gas Mark 6) for 20 minutes.

Scatter over the cheese and bake for a further 5 minutes or until the cheese has melted and is golden.

Serves 2 to 4

Chicken à la King Pizza

METRIC/IMPERIAL

1 quantity basic scone pizza dough
25 g/1 oz butter or margarine
1 small onion, finely chopped
100 g/4 oz small button mushrooms
25 g/1 oz flour
300 ml/½ pint milk
175 g/6 oz cooked chicken meat, diced
1 tablespoon chopped pimento
salt
freshly ground black pepper
1 tablespoon medium sherry
50 g/2 oz fresh breadcrumbs

AMERICAN

1 quantity basic biscuit pizza dough
2 tablespoons butter or margarine
1 small onion, finely chopped
¼ lb small button mushrooms
¼ cup flour
1¼ cups milk
¾ cup diced cooked chicken meat
1 tablespoon chopped pimiento
salt
freshly ground black pepper
1 tablespoon medium sherry
1 cup fresh breadcrumbs

Roll out the dough to one large or two smaller rounds about 1 cm/½ inch thick. Transfer to a greased baking sheet, and push up the edge of the round(s) to make a rim.

Melt the butter or margarine in a saucepan, add the onion and fry until softened. Add the mushrooms and fry until just tender. Remove the mushrooms with a slotted spoon. Stir the flour into the onion and fat and cook for 1 minute, then gradually stir in the milk. Bring to the boil, stirring. Fold in the chicken and pimento and season to taste with salt and pepper. Return the mushrooms to the mixture. Stir in the sherry.

Spread the chicken mixture over the dough round(s) and scatter with the breadcrumbs. Bake in a preheated moderately hot oven (200°C/400°F, Gas Mark 6) for 20 to 25 minutes or until golden brown.

Serves 2 to 4

Quick variation:
Use 1 × 418 g/10 oz can chicken suprême (1 × 10 oz can chicken à la king) and 1 × 213 g/7½ oz can mushrooms, drained.

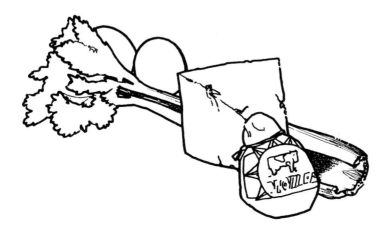

Bacon and Olive Pizza

METRIC/IMPERIAL
1 quantity basic scone pizza dough
1 quantity tomato sauce
6 streaky bacon rashers, rinded
50 g/2 oz Cheddar cheese, grated
3 pimento-stuffed olives, halved
parsley sprig to garnish

AMERICAN
1 quantity basic biscuit pizza dough
1 quantity tomato sauce
6 bacon slices
½ cup grated Cheddar cheese
3 pimiento-stuffed olives, halved
parsley sprig to garnish

Roll out the dough to one large or two smaller rounds about 1 cm/½ inch thick. Transfer to a greased baking sheet and push up the edge of the round(s) to make a rim.

Spread the tomato sauce over the dough round(s), then arrange the bacon on top like the spokes of a wheel. Sprinkle over the cheese and garnish with the olive halves. Bake in a preheated moderately hot oven (200°C/400°F, Gas Mark 6) for 20 to 25 minutes. Garnish with a parsley sprig.

Serves 2 to 4

Bacon and Sweetcorn Pizza

METRIC/IMPERIAL
1 quantity basic scone pizza dough
1 tablespoon oil
100 g/4 oz back bacon, in the piece,
  derinded and chopped
1 × 326 g/11½ oz can sweetcorn,
  drained
salt
freshly ground black pepper
100 g/4 oz Double Gloucester cheese,
  grated

AMERICAN
1 quantity basic biscuit pizza dough
1 tablespoon oil
¼ lb Canadian bacon, chopped
1 × 11½ oz can corn kernels,
  drained
salt
freshly ground black pepper
1 cup grated brick cheese

Roll out the dough to one large or two smaller rounds about 1 cm/½ inch thick. Transfer to a greased baking sheet, and push up the edge of the round(s) to make a rim.

Heat the oil in a frying pan (skillet), add the bacon and fry until it is browned and cooked through. Drain well and mix with the sweetcorn and salt and pepper to taste. Spread over the dough round(s) and scatter with the cheese. Bake in a preheated moderately hot oven (200°C/400°F, Gas Mark 6) for 20 to 25 minutes.

Serves 2 to 4

BACON AND OLIVE PIZZA *(Photograph: Flour Advisory Bureau)*

Pizza Bolognese

METRIC/IMPERIAL

4 tablespoons olive oil

100 g/4 oz lean back bacon, derinded
  and diced

1 onion, finely chopped

1 garlic clove, crushed

1 carrot, diced

1 celery stalk, diced

225 g/8 oz minced beef

150 ml/¼ pint dry white wine

150 ml/¼ pint beef stock

4 tablespoons tomato purée

salt

freshly ground black pepper

1 quantity basic yeast pizza dough

75 g/3 oz Fontina cheese, cut into
  strips

AMERICAN

¼ cup olive oil

¼ lb Canadian bacon, diced

1 onion, finely chopped

1 garlic clove, crushed

1 carrot, diced

1 celery stalk, diced

½ lb ground beef

⅔ cup dry white wine

⅔ cup beef stock

¼ cup tomato paste

salt

freshly ground black pepper

1 quantity basic yeast pizza dough

3 oz Fontina cheese, cut into strips

Heat the oil in a saucepan, add the bacon, onion, garlic, carrot and celery and fry until the vegetables are beginning to soften. Stir in the beef and brown well. Add the wine, stock, tomato purée (paste) and salt and pepper to taste and bring to the boil. Simmer for about 25 minutes or until the sauce is thick.

Meanwhile, roll out the risen dough to one large or two smaller rounds about 1 cm/½ inch thick and transfer to a greased baking sheet. Push up the edge of the round(s) to make a rim. Leave in a warm place to rise for 10 to 15 minutes, then bake in a preheated moderately hot oven (200°C/400°F, Gas Mark 6) for 15 minutes.

Spread the sauce over the pizza base and arrange the cheese strips on top. Return to the oven and bake for a further 15 to 20 minutes.

Serves 2 to 4

Spicy Lamb Pizza

METRIC/IMPERIAL	AMERICAN
25 g/1 oz butter or margarine	2 tablespoons butter or margarine
1 tablespoon oil	1 tablespoon oil
1 onion, chopped	1 onion, chopped
1 garlic clove, crushed	1 garlic clove, crushed
225 g/8 oz cooked lamb, minced	1 cup ground cooked lamb
1 teaspoon ground cinnamon or allspice	1 teaspoon ground cinnamon or allspice
$\frac{1}{2}$ teaspoon ground cumin	$\frac{1}{2}$ teaspoon ground cumin
salt	salt
freshly ground black pepper	freshly ground black pepper
3 tablespoons tomato purée	3 tablespoons tomato paste
1 quantity basic yeast pizza dough	1 quantity basic yeast pizza dough

Melt the butter or margarine with the oil in a frying pan (skillet), add the onion and garlic and fry until softened. Stir in the lamb and brown well, then add the spices, salt and pepper to taste and the tomato purée (paste). Moisten with a little water and mix well. Simmer until the mixture is thick.

Meanwhile, roll out the risen dough to one large or two smaller rounds about 1 cm/$\frac{1}{2}$ inch thick and transfer to a greased baking sheet. Push up the edge of the round(s) to make a rim.

Spread the lamb mixture over the dough round(s). Leave in a warm place to rise for 10 to 15 minutes, then bake in a preheated moderately hot oven (200°C/400°F, Gas Mark 6) for 30 to 35 minutes.

Serves 2 to 4

FISH AND SHELLFISH PIZZAS

Sardine and Fried Cheese Pizza

METRIC/IMPERIAL
225 g/8 oz self-raising flour
1 teaspoon baking powder
1 teaspoon dry mustard
¼ teaspoon salt
pinch of cayenne pepper
50 g/2 oz butter or margarine
100 g/4 oz cheese, grated
about 7 tablespoons milk
Topping:
2 tablespoons oil
1 quantity tomato sauce
1 × 100 g/4 oz can sardines in oil,
  drained
50 g/2 oz cheese, grated
½ teaspoon dried thyme
2 spring onions, chopped (optional)

AMERICAN
2 cups self-rising flour
1 teaspoon baking powder
1 teaspoon dry mustard
¼ teaspoon salt
pinch of cayenne pepper
4 tablespoons butter or margarine
1 cup grated cheese
about 7 tablespoons milk
Topping:
2 tablespoons oil
1 quantity tomato sauce
1 × ¼ lb can sardines in oil,
  drained
½ cup grated cheese
½ teaspoon dried thyme
2 scallions, chopped (optional)

Sift the flour, baking powder, mustard, salt and cayenne into a bowl. Rub in the butter or margarine followed by the cheese, then bind to a soft dough with the milk. Roll out the dough to a round about 1 cm/½ inch thick.

Heat the oil in a frying pan (skillet) large enough to take the dough round, put the dough into the pan and cook until the underside is golden brown. Turn over and cook the other side until golden.

Spread the tomato sauce over the dough round. Arrange the sardines over the top and sprinkle with the cheese, thyme and spring onions (scallions), if using. Place under a preheated grill (broiler) and cook until the cheese has melted and is bubbling.

Serves 2 to 4

SARDINE AND FRIED CHEESE PIZZA *(Photograph: John West Foods)*

Tuna and Pear Pizza

METRIC/IMPERIAL
1 × 200 g/7 oz can tuna fish
1 Spanish onion, chopped
2 ripe dessert pears, peeled, cored
  and chopped
1 × 225 g/8 oz can tomatoes
½ teaspoon dried oregano
salt
freshly ground black pepper
1 quantity basic yeast pizza dough
8 anchovy fillets
9 pickled walnuts or black olives

AMERICAN
1 × 7 oz can tuna fish
1 Bermuda onion, chopped
2 ripe dessert pears, peeled, cored
  and chopped
1 × ½ lb can tomatoes
½ teaspoon dried oregano
salt
freshly ground black pepper
1 quantity basic yeast pizza dough
8 anchovy fillets
9 pickled walnuts or black olives

Drain the oil from the can of tuna into a saucepan, add the onion and pears and cook until the onion is beginning to soften. Flake the tuna and add to the pan with the tomatoes. Simmer for about 25 minutes or until most of the liquid has evaporated. Stir in the oregano and salt and pepper to taste, then cool slightly.

Roll out the risen dough to one large or two smaller rounds about 1 cm/½ inch thick and transfer to a greased baking sheet. Push up the edge of the round(s) to make a rim. Spread the tuna mixture over the dough round(s) and arrange the anchovy fillets and walnuts or olives on top. Leave in a warm place to rise for 10 to 15 minutes.

Bake in a preheated moderately hot oven (200°C/400°F, Gas Mark 6) for 30 to 35 minutes.

Serves 2 to 4

Tomato Tuna Pizza

METRIC/IMPERIAL

1 × 300 g/10 oz packet white bread
 or 1 quantity basic yeast pizza
 dough
1 teaspoon paprika
2 tablespoons tomato purée
25 g/1 oz butter or margarine
1 large onion, sliced
1 × 200 g/7 oz can tuna fish, drained
 and flaked
175 g/6 oz Cheddar cheese, grated
salt
freshly ground black pepper

AMERICAN

1 × 10 oz package white bread mix,
 or 1 quantity basic yeast pizza
 dough
1 teaspoon paprika
2 tablespoons tomato paste
2 tablespoons butter or margarine
1 large onion, sliced
1 × 7 oz can tuna fish, drained and
 flaked
1½ cups grated Cheddar cheese
salt
freshly ground black pepper

If using bread mix, add the paprika to the dry mix, then make up according to the instructions on the package, dissolving the tomato purée (paste) in the hot water used to make the dough. Knead for 5 minutes. Add the paprika to the yeast dough with the salt, and the tomato purée (paste) with the yeast liquid. Roll out the dough to one large or two smaller rounds about 1 cm/½ inch thick. Transfer to a greased baking sheet and push up the edge of the round(s) to make a rim. Leave to rise in a warm place for 30 minutes.

Meanwhile, melt the butter or margarine in a frying pan (skillet), add the onion and fry until softened. Drain the onion.

Spread the onion over the dough round(s), then scatter over the tuna and cover with the cheese. Season to taste with salt and pepper. Bake the bread mix pizza in a preheated hot oven (220°C/425°F, Gas Mark 7) for 20 minutes; use a moderately hot oven (200°C/400°F, Gas Mark 6) for a yeast dough pizza, and bake for 30 to 35 minutes.

Serves 2 to 4

Fried Mackerel and Tomato Pizza

METRIC/IMPERIAL
225 g/8 oz self-raising flour
salt
freshly ground black pepper
100 g/4 oz shredded suet
1 teaspoon dried mixed herbs
150 ml/¼ pint water
fat for frying
Topping:
25 g/1 oz butter or margarine
1 onion, chopped
1 × 225 g/8 oz can tomatoes, drained
½ × 340 g/11½ oz can condensed
  tomato soup
1 garlic clove, crushed (optional)
1 × 198 g/7 oz can mackerel in
  natural juices, drained, boned and
  broken into pieces
Garnish:
watercress
lemon slices

AMERICAN
2 cups self-rising flour
salt
freshly ground black pepper
½ cup shredded suet
1 teaspoon dried mixed herbs
⅔ cup water
fat for frying
Topping:
2 tablespoons butter or margarine
1 onion, chopped
1 × ½ lb can tomatoes, drained
½ × 11½ oz can condensed tomato
  soup
1 garlic clove, crushed (optional)
1 × 7 oz can mackerel in natural
  juices, drained, boned and broken
  into pieces
Garnish:
watercress
lemon slices

Sift the flour into a bowl and add salt and pepper to taste. Stir in the suet and herbs, then bind to a soft dough with the water. Knead lightly. Roll out the dough to a 25 cm/10 inch round. Heat the fat in a frying pan (skillet) large enough to take the dough round, add the dough round and fry gently until lightly browned on the underside. Turn over and brown the other side.

Meanwhile, make the topping. Melt the butter or margarine in a saucepan, add the onion and fry until softened. Stir in the tomatoes, undiluted soup, the garlic, if used, and salt and pepper to taste. Cook for 5 minutes.

Slide the pizza base out of the pan onto a heated serving dish. Spread over the tomato topping and arrange the mackerel pieces on top. Garnish with watercress and lemon slices.

Serves 4 to 6

FRIED MACKEREL AND TOMATO PIZZA *(Photograph: Canned Food Advisory Service)*

Sardine and Caper Pizza

METRIC/IMPERIAL
1 quantity basic scone pizza dough
1 quantity tomato sauce
2 × 100 g/4 oz cans sardines in oil,
  drained
2 tablespoons capers
8 black olives, halved and stoned
freshly ground black pepper

AMERICAN
1 quantity basic biscuit pizza dough
1 quantity tomato sauce
2 × ¼ lb cans sardines in oil,
  drained
2 tablespoons capers
8 black olives, halved and pitted
freshly ground black pepper

Roll out the dough to one large or two smaller rounds about 1 cm/½ inch
thick. Transfer to a greased baking sheet and push up the edge of the
round(s) to make a rim.

Spread the dough with the tomato sauce, then arrange the sardines on
top. Scatter over the capers and olives and sprinkle with black pepper.

Bake in a preheated moderately hot oven (200°C/400°F, Gas Mark 6)
for 20 to 25 minutes.
Serves 2 to 4

Anchovy and Curried Egg Pizza

METRIC/IMPERIAL
1 quantity basic scone pizza dough
75 g/3 oz cheese, grated
1 × 50 g/2 oz can anchovy fillets,
  drained
4 hard-boiled eggs, sliced
½ to 1 teaspoon mild curry powder
salt
freshly ground black pepper
4 tomatoes, thinly sliced

AMERICAN
1 quantity basic biscuit pizza dough
¾ cup grated cheese
1 × 2 oz can anchovy fillets,
  drained
4 hard-cooked eggs, sliced
½ to 1 teaspoon mild curry powder
salt
freshly ground black pepper
4 tomatoes, thinly sliced

Roll out the dough to one large or two smaller rounds about 1 cm/½ inch
thick and transfer to a greased baking sheet. Push up the edge of the
round(s) to make a rim. Sprinkle 25 g/1 oz (¼ cup) of the cheese over the
round(s), then bake in a preheated moderately hot oven (200°C/400°F,
Gas Mark 6) for 15 minutes.

Arrange the anchovies on the base and cover with the egg slices.
Sprinkle with the curry powder and salt and pepper to taste. Top with the
tomato slices and scatter over remaining cheese. Bake for a further 5 to 10
minutes.
Serves 2 to 4

Celery, Brisling and Tomato Pizza

METRIC/IMPERIAL
1 quantity basic yeast pizza dough
1 tablespoon oil
50 g/2 oz Mozzarella cheese,
  thinly sliced
2 teaspoons tomato purée
2 tomatoes, sliced
2 celery stalks, sliced
1 × 65 g/2½ oz can brisling in oil,
  drained
few halved and stoned black olives
  to garnish

AMERICAN
1 quantity basic yeast pizza dough
1 tablespoon oil
2 oz Mozzarella cheese, thinly
  sliced
2 teaspoons tomato paste
2 tomatoes, sliced
2 celery stalks, sliced
1 × 2½ oz can brisling in oil,
  drained
few halved and pitted black olives to
  garnish

Roll out the risen dough to one large or two smaller rounds about 1 cm/½ inch thick. Transfer to a greased baking sheet and push up the edge of the round(s) to make a rim.

Brush the dough with a little of the oil, then cover the round(s) with half the cheese slices. Spread with the tomato purée (paste). Arrange the tomato slices around the edge and pile the celery in the centre. Place the brisling in a ring on the tomato slices. Top with the remaining cheese and dribble over the remaining oil. Leave to rise in a warm place for 10 to 15 minutes.

Bake in a moderately hot oven (200°C/400°F, Gas Mark 6) for 30 to 35 minutes. Garnish with a few olives.

Serves 2

Tomato and Brisling Pizza Tart

METRIC/IMPERIAL
shortcrust pastry dough made with
  175 g/6 oz flour
2 × 100 g/4 oz cans brisling, drained
salt
freshly ground black pepper
juice of ½ lemon
1 quantity tomato sauce
Garnish:
16 pimento-stuffed olives
parsley to garnish

AMERICAN
pie pastry dough made with 1½ cups
  flour
2 × ¼ lb cans brisling, drained
salt
freshly ground black pepper
juice of ½ lemon
1 quantity tomato sauce
Garnish:
16 pimiento-stuffed olives
parsley to garnish

Roll out the dough and use to line a 20 cm/8 inch flan ring (shallow pie pan). Bake blind (unfilled) in a preheated moderately hot oven (200°C/ 400°F, Gas Mark 6) for 25 to 30 minutes. Cool.

Mash half the brisling with salt and pepper to taste and the lemon juice. Spread out in the pastry case. Cover with the tomato sauce. Arrange the remaining brisling on top like the spokes of a wheel, and garnish with the olives and parsley. Serve warm or cold.

Serves 4 to 6

TOMATO AND BRISLING PIZZA TART *(Photograph: John West Foods)*

Shrimp Pizza

METRIC/IMPERIAL

1 small onion, finely chopped
150 ml/¼ pint dry white wine
225 g/8 oz cooked peeled shrimps
225 g/8 oz mushrooms, chopped
25 g/1 oz butter or margarine
25 g/1 oz flour
300 ml/½ pint chicken stock
1 garlic clove, crushed
2 teaspoons tomato purée
4 tomatoes, skinned, seeded and
 chopped
salt
freshly ground black pepper
1 quantity basic yeast pizza dough

AMERICAN

1 small onion, finely chopped
⅔ cup dry white wine
½ lb cooked shelled shrimps
2 cups chopped mushrooms
2 tablespoons butter or margarine
¼ cup flour
1¼ cups chicken stock
1 garlic clove, crushed
2 teaspoons tomato paste
4 tomatoes, skinned, seeded and
 chopped
salt
freshly ground black pepper
1 quantity basic yeast pizza dough

Put the onion and wine in a saucepan and bring to the boil. Simmer until reduced by half. Add the shrimps and mushrooms and continue simmering for 5 minutes.

Meanwhile, melt the butter or margarine in another saucepan, add the flour and cook, stirring, for 2 minutes. Gradually stir in the stock and bring to the boil. Add the garlic and tomato purée (paste) and simmer, stirring, until thickened. Stir in the shrimp mixture and the tomatoes and season to taste with salt and pepper. Remove from the heat.

Roll out the risen dough to one large or two smaller rounds about 1 cm/½ inch thick and transfer to a greased baking sheet. Push up the edge of the round(s) to make a rim. Spread over the shrimp mixture and leave in a warm place to rise for 10 to 15 minutes.

Bake in a preheated moderately hot oven (200°C/400°F, Gas Mark 6) for 30 to 35 minutes.

Serves 2 to 4

Pizza alle Vongole

METRIC/IMPERIAL
1 quantity basic yeast pizza dough
double quantity tomato sauce
25 g/1 oz butter or margarine
15 g/½ oz flour
4 tablespoons dry white wine
120 ml/4 fl oz double cream
1 × 225 g/8 oz can clams, drained
  and chopped
salt
freshly ground black pepper

AMERICAN
1 quantity basic yeast pizza dough
double quantity tomato sauce
2 tablespoons butter or margarine
2 tablespoons flour
¼ cup dry white wine
½ cup heavy cream
1 × ½ lb can clams, drained and
  chopped
salt
freshly ground black pepper

Roll out the risen dough to one large or two smaller rounds about
1 cm/½ inch thick and transfer to a greased baking sheet. Push up the edge
of the round(s) to make a rim. Spread over the tomato sauce, then leave
in a warm place to rise for 10 to 15 minutes.

Bake in a preheated moderately hot oven (200°C/400°F, Gas Mark 6)
for 30 to 35 minutes.

Meanwhile, melt the butter or margarine in a saucepan, stir in the flour
and cook for 1 minute. Gradually stir in the wine followed by the cream
and bring to the boil. Add the clams and salt and pepper to taste and heat
through gently, stirring well.

Spoon the clam sauce over the hot pizza and serve.

Serves 2 to 4

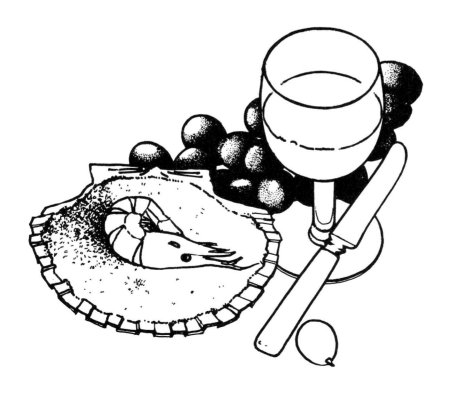

Neapolitan Pizza

METRIC/IMPERIAL

1 quantity basic yeast pizza dough
4 tablespoons olive oil
350 g/12 oz tomatoes, skinned and
  sliced
salt
freshly ground black pepper
1 tablespoon chopped fresh basil or
  1 teaspoon dried basil
1 teaspoon dried oregano
175 g/6 oz Mozzarella or Bel Paese
  cheese, thinly sliced
25 g/1 oz Parmesan cheese, grated
50 g/2 oz mushrooms, sliced
6 anchovy fillets
8 black olives

AMERICAN

1 quantity basic yeast pizza dough
$\frac{1}{4}$ cup olive oil
$\frac{3}{4}$ lb tomatoes, skinned and sliced
salt
freshly ground black pepper
1 tablespoon chopped fresh basil or
  1 teaspoon dried basil
1 teaspoon dried oregano
6 oz Mozzarella or Bel Paese cheese,
  thinly sliced
$\frac{1}{4}$ cup grated Parmesan cheese
$\frac{1}{2}$ cup sliced mushrooms
6 anchovy fillets
8 black olives

Roll out the risen dough to one large or two smaller rounds about
1 cm/$\frac{1}{2}$ inch thick and transfer to a greased baking sheet. Push up the edge
of the round(s) to make a rim.

Sprinkle 2 tablespoons of the oil over the dough round(s), then cover
with the tomato slices. Sprinkle with salt and pepper, the basil and
oregano. Place the cheese slices on top and sprinkle with the Parmesan.
Arrange the mushrooms, anchovies and olives on top of the cheese.
Sprinkle with the remaining oil. Leave in a warm place to rise for 10 to 15
minutes.

Bake in a preheated moderately hot oven (200°C/400°F, Gas Mark 6)
for 30 to 35 minutes.
Serves 2 to 4

NEAPOLITAN PIZZA *(Photographer: Bob Golden)*

SMALL PIZZAS

Mini Salami Pizzas

METRIC/IMPERIAL	AMERICAN
1 × 300 g/10 oz packet brown bread mix, or 1 quantity basic yeast pizza dough	1 × 10 oz package brown bread mix, or 1 quantity basic yeast pizza dough
1 tablespoon oil	1 tablespoon oil
1 × 400 g/14 oz can tomatoes, drained and chopped	1 × 14 oz can tomatoes, drained and chopped
175 g/6 oz Cheddar cheese, grated	1½ cups grated Cheddar cheese
100 g/4 oz salami, thinly sliced	¼ lb salami, thinly sliced
1 processed cheese slice, quartered	1 processed cheese slice, quartered
20 black olives	20 black olives

If using bread mix, make it up according to the instructions on the package and knead for 5 minutes. Divide the dough into four portions and roll out to 15 cm/6 inch rounds. Push up the edge of the rounds to make a rim. Transfer the rounds to a greased baking sheet.

Brush the dough rounds with the oil, then scatter over the tomatoes followed by the grated cheese. Arrange the salami slices around the edge and place a processed cheese quarter in the centre. Top with 5 black olives to each pizza. Leave in a warm place to rise – about 15 minutes for yeast dough and 30 minutes for bread mix.

Bake in a preheated moderately hot oven (200°C/400°F, Gas Mark 6) for about 20 minutes.
Makes 4

Antipasto Pizzas

METRIC/IMPERIAL
1 quantity basic yeast pizza dough
1 quantity tomato sauce
½ pepperoni sausage, sliced
6 green olives
7 black olives
1 to 2 tablespoons capers
2 tablespoons grated Parmesan cheese
4 salami slices
2 processed cheese slices
4 Mozzarella cheese slices
8 anchovy fillets
Garnish:
parsley sprigs
½ pimento-stuffed olive

AMERICAN
1 quantity basic yeast pizza dough
1 quantity tomato sauce
½ pepperoni sausage, sliced
6 green olives
7 black olives
1 to 2 tablespoons capers
2 tablespoons grated Parmesan cheese
4 salami slices
2 processed cheese slices
4 Mozzarella cheese slices
8 anchovy fillets
Garnish:
parsley sprigs
½ pimiento-stuffed olive

Divide the risen dough into four portions and roll out each to a round about 1 cm/½ inch thick. Transfer to greased baking sheets. Push up the edge of each round to make a rim.

Spread the tomato sauce over the dough rounds. In the centre of one round, place a slice of pepperoni and surround it with the green olives, six of the black olives and the capers. Sprinkle over the Parmesan cheese.

On the second dough round, arrange the salami slices shaped into cones.

On the third dough round, place the processed cheese slices in the centre and surround with a ring of the remaining pepperoni slices.

On the fourth dough round, place the Mozzarella cheese slices and arrange the anchovies on top with the remaining black olive in the centre. Leave the pizzas to rise in a warm place for 10 to 15 minutes.

Bake in a preheated moderately hot oven (200°C/400°F, Gas Mark 6) for about 25 minutes. Garnish the salami pizza with a small bunch of parsley, and the pepperoni pizza with an olive half.
Makes 4

Party Pizzas with Mushrooms

METRIC/IMPERIAL
1 quantity basic yeast pizza dough
1 quantity tomato sauce
100 g/4 oz Mozzarella cheese,
  thinly sliced
100 g/4 oz button mushrooms
melted butter or margarine
Garnish:
anchovy fillets
pimento-stuffed olives, sliced
salami slices
green and red pepper strips
cooked peeled prawns
capers
cooked ham, cut into strips

AMERICAN
1 quantity basic yeast pizza dough
1 quantity tomato sauce
$\frac{1}{4}$ lb Mozzarella cheese, thinly
  sliced
$\frac{1}{4}$ lb button mushrooms
melted butter or margarine
Garnish:
anchovy fillets
pimiento-stuffed olives, sliced
salami slices
green and red pepper strips
cooked shelled shrimp
capers
cooked ham, cut into strips

Divide the risen dough into eight portions and roll out into thin rounds. Place on a greased baking sheet. Spread the tomato sauce over the rounds and place a slice of cheese on each. Leave to rise in a warm place for 10 to 15 minutes.

Arrange the mushrooms on the pizzas and brush them with melted butter or margarine. Add any of the remaining suggested garnishes, then bake in a preheated moderately hot oven (200°C/400°F, Gas Mark 6) for 15 to 20 minutes.
Makes 8

PARTY PIZZAS WITH MUSHROOMS (*Photograph: Mushroom Growers' Association*)

Pizza Slices

METRIC/IMPERIAL
1 × 250 g/9 oz packet soft bread roll mix
1 garlic clove, crushed
175 g/6 oz German sausage such as
  bierwurst, diced
75 g/3 oz cheese, grated
1 × 400 g/14 oz can tomatoes,
  drained and chopped
Garnish:
lemon twists
parsley sprigs

AMERICAN
2¼ cups biscuit mix
1 garlic clove, crushed
6 oz German sausage such as
  bierwurst, diced (about ¾ cup)
¾ cup grated cheese
1 × 14 oz can tomatoes, drained and
  chopped
Garnish:
lemon twists
parsley sprigs

Make up the bread roll (biscuit) mix according to the instructions on the package. Mix in the garlic and knead for 5 minutes. Roll out the dough to a 25 × 30 cm/10 × 12 inch rectangle. Transfer to a greased baking sheet, and push up the edge of the rectangle to make a rim. Mark the rim with a fork.

Sprinkle the sausage and cheese over the dough, then scatter over the tomatoes.

Bake in a preheated moderately hot oven (200°C/400°F, Gas Mark 6) for 25 minutes. Cut into four and serve garnished with lemon twists and parsley.

Serves 4

Pizza Canapés

METRIC/IMPERIAL
double quantity basic yeast pizza dough
175 g/6 oz salami, thinly sliced
5 large tomatoes, thinly sliced
2 teaspoons dried oregano
300 to 350 g/10 to 12 oz Cheddar
  cheese, thinly sliced
pimento-stuffed olives to garnish

AMERICAN
double quantity basic yeast pizza dough
6 oz salami, thinly sliced
5 large tomatoes, thinly sliced
2 teaspoons dried oregano
about ¾ lb Cheddar cheese, thinly
  sliced
pimiento-stuffed olives to garnish

Roll out the risen dough to 1 cm/½ inch thick and cut into 24 rounds, using a 7.5 cm/3 inch cutter. Place the rounds on greased baking sheets. Place a slice of salami on each round, then a slice of tomato and sprinkle with oregano. Top with small slices of cheese. Leave to rise in a warm place for 10 to 15 minutes.

Bake in a preheated moderately hot oven (200°C/400°F, Gas Mark 6) for 20 to 25 minutes. Garnish with the olives. Serve hot or cold.

Makes 24

Egg Pizzas

METRIC/IMPERIAL
1 quantity basic scone pizza dough
1 small onion, grated
3 tablespoons tomato purée
½ teaspoon dried oregano or marjoram
salt
freshly ground black pepper
6 hard-boiled eggs, halved
12 black olives, halved and stoned
350 g/12 oz cheese, grated
3 eggs, beaten
1 teaspoon made mustard

AMERICAN
1 quantity basic biscuit pizza dough
1 small onion, grated
3 tablespoons tomato paste
½ teaspoon dried oregano or marjoram
salt
freshly ground black pepper
6 hard-cooked eggs, halved
12 black olives, halved and pitted
3 cups grated cheese
3 eggs, beaten
1 teaspoon prepared mustard

Roll out the dough and cut into six 10 to 12.5 cm/4 to 5 inch rounds. Transfer to a greased baking sheet.

Mix together the onion, tomato purée, herbs and salt and pepper to taste. Spread over the dough rounds. Arrange the egg halves, cut sides down, on the tomato mixture and surround with the olives.

Combine the cheese, beaten eggs and mustard and spread over the hard-boiled eggs.

Bake in a preheated hot oven (220°C/425°F, Gas Mark 7) for 10 to 15 minutes or until risen and golden brown.
Makes 6

Variations:
This may be made as one large pizza, in which case increase the baking time to about 20 minutes.

Split English muffins may be used in place of the pizza dough.

INSTANT PIZZAS

Chicken Liver Toasts

METRIC/IMPERIAL
75 g/3 oz butter or margarine
1 small shallot, finely chopped
3 to 4 fresh sage leaves
225 g/8 oz chicken livers, trimmed
  and finely chopped
freshly ground black pepper
8 small slices of bread, cut 5 mm/¼ inch
  thick
squeeze of lemon juice
chopped parsley to garnish

AMERICAN
6 tablespoons butter or margarine
1 small shallot, finely chopped
3 to 4 fresh sage leaves
½ lb chicken livers, trimmed and
  finely chopped
freshly ground black pepper
8 small slices of bread, cut ¼ inch
  thick
squeeze of lemon juice
chopped parsley to garnish

Melt 40 g/1½ oz (3 tablespoons) of the butter or margarine in a saucepan, add the shallot and sage leaves and cook gently until the shallot is tender. Discard the sage leaves, then add the chicken livers to the pan with pepper to taste. Fry until the livers are no longer pink, stirring occasionally.

Meanwhile, melt the remaining butter or margarine in a frying pan (skillet). Add the bread slices and fry until golden brown on both sides. Drain on paper towels.

Add the lemon juice to the liver mixture, then spread on the fried bread. Sprinkle with parsley and serve.
Serves 4

CHICKEN LIVER TOASTS (*Photographer: Bob Golden*)

Sardine Toasts

METRIC/IMPERIAL
1 × 100 g/4 oz can sardines
2 tablespoons mayonnaise
2 tablespoons chopped fresh herbs
1 egg yolk
4 slices of bread
4 Cheddar cheese slices
sliced pimento-stuffed olives to garnish

AMERICAN
1 × ¼ lb can sardines
2 tablespoons mayonnaise
2 tablespoons chopped fresh herbs
1 egg yolk
4 slices of bread
4 Cheddar cheese slices
sliced pimiento-stuffed olives to garnish

Mash the sardines with the oil from the can and the mayonnaise. Mix in the herbs and egg yolk. Toast the bread lightly on both sides under the preheated grill (broiler). Spread with the sardine mixture and place a cheese slice on top of each. Return to the heat and continue cooking until the cheese has melted and is bubbling. Garnish with olive slices.
Makes 4

Crab and Tomato Toasts

METRIC/IMPERIAL
100 g/4 oz fresh or canned crabmeat,
 flaked
juice of ½ lemon
2 tablespoons tomato purée
50 g/2 oz butter
salt
freshly ground black pepper
4 slices of bread
4 tomato slices
watercress to garnish

AMERICAN
¼ lb fresh or canned crabmeat,
 flaked
juice of ½ lemon
2 tablespoons tomato paste
4 tablespoons butter
salt
freshly ground black pepper
4 slices of bread
4 tomato slices
watercress to garnish

Mix together the crabmeat, lemon juice, tomato purée (paste), 25 g/1 oz (2 tablespoons) of the butter and salt and pepper to taste.

Cut rounds from the bread slices, using a small saucer as a guide. Toast the bread rounds lightly on both sides. Spread the toast with the rest of the butter or margarine, then pile the crabmeat mixture on top. Put a tomato slice on each round, then return to the heat. Cook for 3 to 4 minutes to heat through. Garnish with watercress.
Serves 4

Anchovy Toasts

METRIC/IMPERIAL
1 × 50 g/2 oz can anchovy fillets,
 finely chopped
1 tablespoon grated onion
2 tablespoons chopped parsley
1 tablespoon lemon juice
4 slices of bread

AMERICAN
1 × 2 oz can anchovy fillets, finely
 chopped
1 tablespoon grated onion
2 tablespoons chopped parsley
1 tablespoon lemon juice
4 slices of bread

Mix together the anchovies with their oil, the onion, parsley and lemon juice. Beat well until the mixture is spreadable.

Toast the bread lightly on both sides under a preheated grill (broiler). Spread the anchovy mixture over the toast and return to the heat. Cook for about 2 minutes. Cut into fingers to serve.
Serves 4

Fisherman's Toasties

METRIC/IMPERIAL
1 × 200 g/7 oz can cod's roe, drained
2 tablespoons mango chutney or
 sweet pickle
4 slices of toasted white bread, crusts
 removed
25 g/1 oz butter margarine
225 g/8 oz button mushrooms, sliced
4 processed cheese slices
watercress to garnish

AMERICAN
1 × 7 oz can cod's roe, drained
2 tablespoons mango chutney or
 sweet pickle relish
4 slices of toasted white bread, crusts
 removed
2 tablespoons butter or margarine
½ lb button mushrooms, sliced
4 processed cheese slices
watercress to garnish

Mash the cod's roe with the chutney or pickle (relish) and spread on the toast. Arrange in the grill (broiler) pan and cook gently under the preheated grill (broiler).

Meanwhile, melt the butter or margarine in a frying pan (skillet), add the mushrooms and fry until just tender. Pile the mushrooms on the toast, then cover each with a slice of cheese. Continue grilling (broiling) until the cheese has melted. Serve garnished with watercress.
Makes 4

Cheese and Bacon Toasts

METRIC/IMPERIAL
8 to 12 back bacon rashers,
  derinded
4 slices of bread
made mustard
8 Samsoe or Cheddar cheese slices

AMERICAN
8 to 12 ordinary or Canadian bacon
  slices
4 slices of bread
prepared mustard
8 Samsoe or Cheddar cheese slices

Arrange the bacon on the rack in the grill (broiler) pan and cook under a preheated grill (broiler). Drain on paper towels and keep hot.

Toast the bread lightly on both sides under the grill (broiler). Spread with the mustard and arrange two slices of cheese on each slice of bread. Return to the heat and cook until the cheese has melted and is bubbling. Top with the bacon and serve.

Serves 2 to 4

Quick Portuguese Pizzas

METRIC/IMPERIAL
2 English muffins, split, or 4 baked
  wholemeal scones
tomato ketchup
1 × 100 g/4 oz can sardines in oil,
  drained
garlic salt
4 processed cheese slices
dried oregano
8 black olives, stoned

AMERICAN
2 English muffins, split, or 4 baked
  wholewheat biscuits
tomato catsup
1 × $\frac{1}{4}$ lb can sardines in oil,
  drained
garlic salt
4 processed cheese slices
dried oregano
8 black olives, pitted

Spread each cut surface of the muffins or the scones (biscuits) with ketchup. Top with sardines and sprinkle with garlic salt. Lay a slice of cheese on top of each. Brush with oil from the sardine can and sprinkle with oregano. Garnish with the olives.

Arrange the pizzas on a greased baking sheet and bake in a preheated moderately hot oven (200°C/400°F, Gas Mark 6) for 15 minutes. Alternatively, the pizzas may be cooked under the grill (broiler) for about 10 minutes.

Makes 4

HAM OR CHICKEN GOUGERE PIZZA *(page 75) (Photograph: Marmite)*

Quick Melba Toast Pizzas

METRIC/IMPERIAL
24 Melba toasts
175 ml/6 fl oz tomato ketchup
about 50 g/2 oz pepperoni sausage,
  thinly sliced
100 g/4 oz Mozzarella cheese,
  shredded
dried oregano

AMERICAN
24 Melba toasts
¾ cup tomato catsup
about 2 oz pepperoni sausage, thinly
  sliced
1 cup shredded Mozzarella cheese
dried oregano

Spread the toasts with the ketchup, then arrange the pepperoni slices on top. Sprinkle over the cheese and oregano.

Arrange the toasts on a baking sheet and bake in a preheated moderately hot oven (200°C/400°F, Gas Mark 6) for about 5 minutes or until the cheese has melted.

Makes 24

Hot Bel Paese Bites

METRIC/IMPERIAL
5 slices of white bread, crusts removed
50 g/2 oz butter or margarine
2 tablespoons olive oil
100 g/4 oz Bel Paese cheese, thinly
  sliced
10 anchovy fillets, halved, to garnish

AMERICAN
5 slices of white bread, crusts removed
4 tablespoons butter or margarine
2 tablespoons olive oil
¼ lb Bel Paese cheese, thinly sliced
10 anchovy fillets, halved, to garnish

Cut each slice of bread into quarters. Melt the butter or margarine with the oil in a frying pan (skillet). Add the bread squares, in batches, and fry until crisp and golden on both sides. Drain on paper towels.

Cut the cheese slices into squares the same size as the bread squares and place one on each bread square. Arrange in the grill (broiler) pan and cook under a preheated grill (broiler) until the cheese has melted. Garnish each square with half an anchovy.

Makes 20

Chicken and Mushroom Rounds

METRIC/IMPERIAL
6 slices of white bread
75 g/3 oz butter or margarine
350 g/12 oz cooked chicken meat,
  thickly sliced
1 small onion, sliced
225 g/8 oz mushrooms, sliced
¼ teaspoon dried mixed herbs
salt
freshly ground black pepper
2 tablespoons fresh breadcrumbs
1 egg, beaten
15 g/1 oz blanched almonds, chopped

AMERICAN
6 slices of white bread
6 tablespoons butter or margarine
¾ lb cooked chicken meat, thickly
  sliced
1 small onion, sliced
½ lb mushrooms, sliced
¼ teaspoon dried mixed herbs
salt
freshly ground black pepper
2 tablespoons fresh breadcrumbs
1 egg, beaten
¼ cup chopped blanched almonds

Cut the bread into six rounds, using a saucer as a guide. Toast the bread lightly and spread one side with 40 g/1½ oz (3 tablespoons) of the butter or margarine. Arrange the rounds, buttered sides up, in a baking dish and place the chicken on the rounds.

Melt the remaining butter or margarine in a frying pan (skillet), add the onion and mushrooms and cook until the onion is softened. Stir in the herbs, salt and pepper to taste and the breadcrumbs, then bind with the egg. Top the chicken with the mushroom mixture and sprinkle with the almonds.

Bake in a preheated moderately hot oven (200°C/400°F, Gas Mark 6) for about 20 minutes.

Makes 6

NEAR PIZZAS

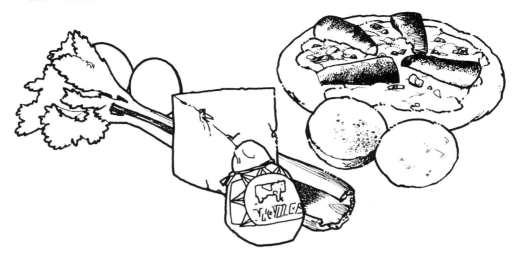

Pancake (Crêpe) Pizzas

METRIC/IMPERIAL
50 g/2 oz flour
pinch of salt
1 small egg, beaten
about 150 ml/¼ pint milk
oil for frying
Topping:
1 × 225 g/8 oz can tomatoes
good pinch of dried mixed herbs
300 ml/½ pint hot thick cheese sauce
1 × 100 g/4 oz can sardines, drained
6 tablespoons grated cheese
14 black olives to garnish

AMERICAN
½ cup flour
pinch of salt
1 small egg, beaten
about ⅔ cup milk
oil for frying
Topping:
1 × ½ lb can tomatoes
large pinch of dried mixed herbs
1¼ cups hot thick cheese sauce
1 × ¼ lb can sardines, drained
6 tablespoons grated cheese
14 black olives to garnish

Sift the flour and salt into a mixing bowl. Add the egg and half the milk and beat until smooth. Gradually stir in the remaining milk to make smooth, pouring batter.

Lightly oil a 25 cm/10 inch frying or pancake (crêpe) pan (skillet) and make 4 thickish pancakes (crêpes). Keep warm.

Tip the tomatoes into a saucepan, add the herbs and heat through. Place a pancake (crêpe) on each of two warmed flameproof serving plates and spread over half the tomatoes. Cover with the remaining pancakes (crêpes). Spread over the cheese sauce, then add the rest of the tomatoes. Arrange the sardines on top and sprinkle with the cheese.

Cook under a preheated grill (broiler) until the cheese has melted and is starting to brown. Garnish with the olives.
Serves 2

PANCAKE (CREPE) PIZZA *(Photograph: John West Foods)*

Pasta Pizza

METRIC/IMPERIAL
100 g/4 oz short-cut pasta
  (macaroni, shells, etc.)
salt
40 g/1½ oz butter or margarine
1 onion, finely chopped
4 eggs
6 tablespoons milk
freshly ground black pepper
3 tomatoes, sliced
4 tablespoons tomato ketchup
75 g/3 oz cheese, thinly sliced
Garnish:
6 anchovy fillets
9 black olives

AMERICAN
¼ lb short-cut pasta (macaroni,
  shells, etc.)
salt
3 tablespoons butter or margarine
1 onion, finely chopped
4 eggs
6 tablespoons milk
freshly ground black pepper
3 tomatoes, sliced
¼ cup tomato catsup
3 oz cheese, thinly sliced
Garnish:
6 anchovy fillets
9 black olives

Cook the pasta in boiling salted water until it is just tender. Drain well.

Melt the butter or margarine in a large frying pan (skillet), add the onion and fry until softened. Beat the eggs with the milk and salt and pepper to taste. Fold in the pasta. Pour the egg and pasta mixture into the pan and cook gently, stirring occasionally so that the liquid egg mixture can run onto the pan. When the mixture has just set, arrange the tomato slices over the top. Spoon over the ketchup and cover with the cheese.

Place the pan under a preheated grill (broiler) and cook until the pizza 'rises' and the cheese is bubbling. Garnish with the anchovies and olives.
Serves 4 to 6

Sweetcorn and Broad (Lima) Bean Fritter Pizza

Fritter batter:

1 × 198 g/7 oz can sweetcorn kernels
  with peppers
1 egg, beaten
50 g/2 oz self-raising flour, sifted
pinch of salt
2 tablespoons milk
oil for frying

Topping:

40 g/1½ oz butter or margarine
40 g/1½ oz flour
1 × 284 g/11 oz can broad beans
300 ml/½ pint milk
2 tablespoons chopped parsley
freshly ground black pepper

Garnish:

4 streaky bacon rashers, rinded and
  halved lengthways
parsley sprigs

AMERICAN

Fritter batter:

1 × 7 oz can corn kernels with
  peppers
1 egg, beaten
½ cup self-rising flour, sifted
pinch of salt
2 tablespoons milk
oil for frying

Topping:

3 tablespoons butter or margarine
6 tablespoons flour
1 × 11 oz can lima beans
1¼ cups milk
2 tablespoons chopped parsley
freshly ground black pepper

Garnish:

8 bacon slices
parsley sprigs

First make the batter. Mix together the undrained sweetcorn, the egg, flour, salt and milk. Set aside.

Melt the butter or margarine in a saucepan, stir in the flour and cook for 2 minutes. Drain the beans and add enough of the liquid to the milk to make it up to 450 ml/¾ pint (1 pint). Gradually add the liquid to the pan, stirring well, and bring to the boil. Simmer until thickened. Stir in the beans, parsley and pepper to taste. Remove from the heat and keep warm.

Cook the bacon under a preheated grill (broiler). Meanwhile, heat the oil in a fairly large frying pan, pour in the fritter batter and cook until brown on both sides.

Slide the fritter onto a heated serving dish and spoon the bean sauce over the top. Garnish with a lattice of bacon and parsley sprig.

Serves 4 to 6

Bubble and Squeak Pizza

METRIC/IMPERIAL
500 g/1 lb potatoes, cooked and mashed
225 g/8 oz cabbage, cored, chopped
  and cooked
salt
freshly ground black pepper
50 g/2 oz butter or margarine
1 tablespoon oil
1 small onion, chopped
1 × 220 g/7¾ oz can baked beans
1 × 170 g/6 oz can bacon grill, cubed
1 tablespoon chutney
1 teaspoon Worcestershire sauce
parsley sprig to garnish

AMERICAN
1 lb potatoes, cooked and mashed
½ lb cabbage, cored, chopped and
  cooked
salt
freshly ground black pepper
4 tablespoons butter or margarine
1 tablespoon oil
1 small onion, chopped
1 × 7¾ oz can baked beans
½ lb cooked ham or canned meat, cubed
1 tablespoon chutney
1 teaspoon Worcestershire sauce
parsley sprig to garnish

Mix together the potatoes and cabbage and season with salt and pepper.
Melt the butter or margarine in a fairly large frying pan (skillet) and
spread out the potato mixture in an even layer in the pan. Cook gently
until the underside is golden brown, then turn over carefully and brown
the other side. This will take 15 to 20 minutes altogether.

Meanwhile, heat the oil in a saucepan, add the onion and fry until
softened. Stir in the beans, meat, chutney and Worcestershire sauce and
heat through gently.

Slide the pizza base onto a heated serving dish and spoon the bean
mixture on top. Garnish with parsley.

Serves 2 to 4

BUBBLE AND SQUEAK PIZZA *(Photograph: Canned Food
Advisory Service)*

Beef and Rice Pizza

METRIC/IMPERIAL	AMERICAN
225 g/8 oz long-grain rice	1 cup long-grain rice
2 eggs, beaten	2 eggs, beaten
225 g/8 oz Mozzarella cheese, shredded	½ lb Mozzarella cheese, shredded
500 g/1 lb minced beef	1 lb ground beef
1 onion, chopped	1 onion, chopped
1 garlic clove, crushed	1 garlic clove, crushed
1 quantity tomato sauce	1 quantity tomato sauce
2 tomatoes, sliced	2 tomatoes, sliced
2 tablespoons grated Parmesan cheese	2 tablespoons grated Parmesan cheese

Cook the rice in boiling water until it is tender. Drain if necessary, then allow to cool slightly. Beat in the eggs and half the Mozzarella cheese. Press the rice mixture evenly over the bottom and sides of a greased shallow 30 cm/12 inch pizza pan (or two smaller pans). Bake in a preheated hot oven (230°C/450°F, Gas Mark 8) for 20 minutes.

Meanwhile, put the beef, onion and garlic in a dry frying pan (skillet) and fry until the beef is browned and crumbly. Drain off all the fat, then stir in the tomato sauce.

Pour the beef mixture into the rice crust. Arrange the tomato slices on top and scatter over the remaining Mozzarella cheese. Sprinkle with the Parmesan cheese. Return to the oven and bake for a further 10 to 12 minutes or until the cheese has melted and is golden.

Serves 4 to 6

Ham or Chicken Gougère Pizza

METRIC/IMPERIAL

15 g/½ oz butter or margarine
1 large onion, chopped
50 g/2 oz mushrooms, sliced
1 tablespoon flour
1 tablespoon yeast extract
300 ml/½ pint hot water
1 teaspoon dried mixed herbs
100 g/4 oz cooked ham or chicken,
  chopped
Pastry:
150 ml/¼ pint water
1 teaspoon yeast extract
50 g/2 oz butter or margarine
65 g/2½ oz flour, sifted
2 eggs, beaten

AMERICAN

1 tablespoon butter or margarine
1 large onion, chopped
½ cup sliced mushrooms
1 tablespoon flour
1 tablespoon brewer's yeast
1¼ cups hot water
1 teaspoon dried mixed herbs
½ cup chopped cooked ham or
  chicken
Pastry:
⅔ cup water
1 teaspoon brewer's yeast
4 tablespoons butter or margarine
½ cup plus 2 tablespoons flour, sifted
2 eggs, beaten

Melt the butter or margarine in a saucepan, add the onion and fry until softened. Add the mushrooms and fry until just tender, then stir in the flour. Dissolve the yeast extract (brewer's yeast) in the water and add to the pan with the herbs. Bring to the boil, stirring well, and simmer for 5 minutes. Stir in the ham or chicken. Remove from the heat and set aside.

For the pastry, put the water, yeast extract (brewer's yeast) and butter or margarine in a saucepan and bring to the boil, stirring to melt the fat. Remove from the heat and add the flour all at once. Beat until the mixture is smooth and leaves the sides of the pan. Cool slightly, then gradually beat in the eggs to make a smooth and glossy dough.

Spoon the dough evenly around the edge of a well-oiled shallow baking dish. Pour the sauce into the centre. Bake in a preheated moderately hot oven (200°C/400°F, Gas Mark 6) for about 35 minutes or until the pastry is well risen and browned.

Serves 3

INDEX

Neapolitan pizza 52
Near pizzas:
  Beef and rice pizza 74
  Bubble and squeak pizza
    72
  Ham or chicken gougère
    pizza 75
  Pancake (crêpe) pizzas 68
  Pasta pizza 70
  Sweetcorn and broad
    (Lima) bean fritter
    pizza 71

Olive:
  Bacon and olive pizza 36
  Herby olive pizza tart 18

Pancake (crêpe) pizzas 68
Pan-fried tomato pizza 18
Party pizzas with
  mushrooms 56
Pasta pizza 70
Pear:
  Tuna and pear pizza 42
Pepper:
  Mushroom and green
    pepper pizza 12
Pepperoni pizza 26
Pizza bolognese 38
Pizza canapés 58
Pizza slices 58
Portuguese pizzas, quick 64
Prosciutto pizza 24

Quick Melba toast pizzas 66
Quick Portuguese pizzas 64

Salami:
  Mini salami pizzas 54
  Salmi and anchovy
    pizza 20
  Salami pastry pizza 31

Sardine:
  Quick Portuguese pizzas
    64
  Sardine and caper pizza 46
  Sardine and fried cheese
    pizza 40
  Sardine toasts 62
Sauce:
  Tomato sauce 11
Sausage:
  Italian sausage pizza 23
  Liver pâté and sausage
    pan pizza 27
  Liver sausage and
    bratwurst pizza 28
  Pepperoni pizza 26
  Sausage and bean pizza 24
  Sausagemeat and cheese
    pizza, layered 22
Scone (biscuit) pizza dough,
  basic 10
Shellfish see Fish and
  Shellfish
Shrimp pizza 50
Small pizzas:
  Antipasto pizzas 55
  Egg pizzas 59
  Mini salami pizzas 54
  Party pizzas with
    mushrooms 56
  Pizza canapés 58
  Pizza slices 58
Spicy lamb pizza 39
Spinach pizza 19
Sweetcorn:
  Bacon and sweetcorn
    pizza 36
  Chicken and sweetcorn
    pizza 34
  Sweetcorn and broad
    (Lima) bean fritter
    pizza 71

Tomato:
  Crab and tomato toasts
    62
  Fried mackerel and
    tomato pizza 44
  Mushroom and tomato
    pizza plait (braid) 16
  Neapolitan pizza 52
  Pan-fried tomato pizza
    18
  Tomato and artichoke
    pizza 14
  Tomato and brisling
    pizza tart 48
  Tomato sauce 11
  Tomato tuna pizza 43
Tuna:
  Tomato tuna pizza 43
  Tuna and pear pizza 42

Vegetable pizzas:
  Aubergine (eggplant)
    pizza 15
  Herby olive pizza
    tart 18
  Mushroom and green
    pepper pizza 12
  Mushroom pizza 14
  Mushroom and tomato
    pizza plait (braid) 16
  Pan-fried tomato pizza
    18
  Spinach pizza 19
  Tomato and artichoke
    pizza 14

Wholemeal scone
  (wholewheat biscuit)
  pizza dough 8

Yeast pizza dough, basic 10
Yeast pizza dough, rich 11